Codependent Cure

The No More Codependency
Recovery Guide For
Obtaining Detachment
From Codependence
Relationships
Jean Harrison, Beattie Grey

Contents

To express our gratitude for your purchase and support, we're excited to give you free access to our exclusive Codependency Toolkit, a special resource reserved for our valued book readers!

Realizing that you are in a codependent relationship is hard enough, but failing to implement the practical techniques provided in this book will prevent you from recovering from your codependency.

This **Codependency Kit** complements the book beautifully, offering practical and effective techniques designed to expedite your journey toward recovery and healing from codependency.

You'll discover:

- **How to Spot Codependent Patterns:** Instantly reveal the inseparable bond keeping you trapped in your relationship through insightful activities and self-reflection questions

- **Master Detachment Techniques:** A simple and easy-to-implement solution for instant & healthy detachment from your partner

- **Speed Your Recovery and Growth:** Practical steps for enhancing your coping skills to establish a healthy routine that expedites the recovery process.

To start breaking deep-rooted codependent patterns and fast-track your recovery, visit **www.BonusGuides.com/ Kit** or scan the QR code in the image above.

If you're an audiobook enthusiast or enjoy having a book narrated to you while reading, then you're in for a treat. You can download the audiobook version of Codependent Cure for FREE ($14.95 price value) just by signing up for a FREE 30-day trial on Audible!

Visit **www.BonusGuides.com/US-Audible** if you're in the US or scan the first QR code in the image above

Visit **www.BonusGuides.com/UK-Audible** if you're in the UK or scan the second QR code in the image above

ONE

Introduction

THIS BOOK DISCUSSES THE topic of codependency, the different role it plays, and how you can free yourself from it. We'll begin by explaining what codependency is, the various forms in which it can manifest itself, how this concept developed in the world of psychiatry, and the different levels in which someone can be codependent.

Next, we'll go through and explain the different types of dysfunction you may find in yourself and those around you, behaviors that may seem like codependency but are just normal emotions, and habits that may be confused with codependency. We will then go through some of the steps you can take to identify whether you or someone you know is displaying codependent behaviors.

Once we've covered exactly what codependency is and how to identify it, we'll go into steps you can take to remove yourself from codependent situations, including a guide to self-care, making boundaries, reversing people-pleasing behaviors, and detaching yourself from codependent relationships.

Like most psychiatric concepts, codependency is very complex in its causes, symptoms, and effects. In almost all cases, the road to codependency begins in childhood. Of course, all children are entirely dependent on others in the first few years of their lives, and many remain very reliant on their families well into young adulthood. But a person who is codependent to the extent that it becomes harmful both to themselves and their family has certain aspects of their life that rely too much on external factors, such as dynamics, substances, rituals, or other people.

We all grow up learning how to depend on others for survival during childhood. These behaviors are natural and, in most cases, do not become detrimental to us in the long run. However, in codependent people, we find that the gradual growth, separation, and independence that occurs in the development of healthy individuals either takes place partially or not at all.

Before we begin, it's important to clarify that no one decides to become codependent. While it may have caused turmoil, heartache, and struggle in your life, remember that the codependent person is never at fault, nor are the people who find themselves in a relationship with them.

Codependency is the product of an unhealthy environment.

If you find yourself or someone close to you struggling with codependency, this book will help you.

Two

What is Codependency?

For someone new to codependency, it can be a little hard to wrap your head around, as it can spread throughout many areas of life. When trying to grasp the concept, it can be helpful to know the basic idea behind codependency and the different ways people use it, such as in relationships and substance abuse. In this chapter, we'll cover the basic definition of codependency, its history, and its severity in different individuals.

Defining Codependency

The first thing we should establish is that codependency is not a diagnosable disease. Rather, it is a pattern of behavior that usually spans many aspects of an individual's life. In short, a codependent person is someone who either cannot function on their own or has a weak sense of personal identity which causes them to base their self-worth, actions, needs, and desires on something else. Usually, when people talk about codependency, they're referring relationships where a partner has an unhealthy focus, obsession, or dependence on their significant other.

Codependent individuals usually come from an environment or upbringing that didn't supply an adequate amount of love, affection, or intimacy (we'll get further into the causes later). They often feel starved of these aspects in their day to day life, so they try to supplement them through other people. Typically, the lack of these needs leads to an inverse effect in which they give them to other people in large amounts. They show those around them a tremendous amount of love, affection, and empathy in hopes that they will receive it back.

Codependents will often become very overbearing to their partners. Often, they will enter relationships with people who have problems, such as an addiction, mental illness, chronic disease, or anything else that might make them less independent individuals. When they enter these relationships, they will often try to fill the "hole" that their partner has as a result of their problems. They try to fix their partners by devoting a large amount of effort in satisfying them and solving their problems.

In trying to solve their partner's problems and fix them, they'll expect the same amount of love, effort, and empathy in return. Of course, they rarely get it. In fact, they're more likely to suffer at the hands of their partner than get an adequate amount of love or affection in return. They go into relationships with a skewed idea of what is ordinary, which is a direct result of their dysfunctional upbringing. In whatever way their parents or care-takers were dysfunctional, they'll find a partner who demonstrates that same kind of behavior. They also have a hard time leaving a toxic relationship. And even if the relationship is not toxic, they will still have difficulty ending it because that means being alone. And being alone again means being deprived of the love they were starved of in their childhood.

A History of Codependency

While the concept of codependency has been present in western thought for a long time, the term "codependency" as we know it today can be traced back to the founding years of Alcoholic Anonymous. The basic idea of the organization was to help people who felt their lives had spiraled out of control due to their consumption of alcohol. Alcoholics Anonymous gave people who wanted to stop their drinking a place they could go to share their stories and seek support from others who had the same issues. The founders of the organization wrote the famous treatise called the "12 Step Program," which was a path they laid out for their members to help them recover from alcohol dependency.

In the process of creating this program, they had to take a step back to analyze the different variables involved in why people drink and continue to drink. One of the problems they identified that caused people to have issues maintaining their sobriety was what has come to be known as codependence.

In the process of developing the 12 Step Program and analyzing the different things that put a person at risk for alcoholism, the developers of the program identified two factors related to the issue of codependency. First was the move towards calling alcoholism a chemical dependency, identifying the person drinking as someone who was "dependent" on alcohol. But it also found problems in the people who were around the alcohol-dependent person. They realized that a person's alcoholism was sometimes inadvertently supported by a person close to them. When someone was taking on the responsibilities of the alcoholic, they themselves became a barrier between the alcoholic and their recovery. These people came to be known as "co-alcoholics," with the prefix "co" meaning together or mutual. When the program began to integrate science and realized that alcoholism, like all other physical addictions, was a physical dependency on a certain chemical, they started calling these people "co-chemically dependent," which was later shortened to just "codependent."

While codependent individuals were at first simply a surrogate of the problems that someone close to them had, the concept of a codependent person took off as its own issue in the 1980s. At this time, the idea of a mental disorder that wasn't purely a result of predetermined brain biology was not a new idea, but it was only around this time that research psychologists started to look at dysfunctional personalities as actual mental disorders. While codependency itself is not a recognized mental disorder, there is a personality disorder that was established in the 1980s, which is called Dependent Personality Disorder. We'll get into how this personality disorder relates to the concept of codependency in the next section of this chapter.

The Freudian idea of the self also influenced the concept of codependency. In a codependent person, the concept of the self is weak and underdeveloped, causing them a need to attach themselves to a person with a complete or dominant personality to reconcile their own self's weakness.

At the same time when codependency was established to be a legitimate mental disorder, the general public was introduced to the concept through a few popular psychology books that came out in the 1980s. Janet G. Woititz wrote and published a book called Adult Children of Alcoholics in 1983. It sold more than two million copies and stayed on the New York Times bestseller list for a little less than a year. In it, she analyzes the problems that stem from growing up in a toxic household with an alcoholic parent and provides steps to help the reader recover from abuse, addiction, trauma, and codependency. This was the first time the mainstream public had been exposed to the concept of codependency. Then, in 1985, Robin Norwood published Women Who Love Too Much, a self-help book which describes how women can remove themselves from relationships where they are highly dependent on their partner, as well as advice on how to avoid this type of dynamic in the future. However, the term codependency as we know it today came from Melody Beattie's book Codependent No More, which was published in 1986. It gave readers a specific strategy for identifying the reasons and emotions behind codependency and how to heal from it.

These books show that, while the term codependency is less than a century old, it has been lodged within western society for much longer. As soon as someone gave it a name and provided readers with a way to heal themselves of it, millions of people went out to buy it. The concept of codependency isn't new; it just took us a long time to understand it.

The Severity of Codependency

Like all problems that are shared by millions of people, the severity of codependent behavior can vary radically from person to person. It can be a small habit that causes you embarrassment occasionally, or it can be a part of you that's rooted deep within and makes your life significantly worse.

Most people are codependent in many aspects of their life. The problem of codependency doesn't come from the existence of certain behaviors in a person's personality, but the degree in which these behaviors are present and how they influence their quality of life. Generally, codependency is the intense need for acceptance, approval, and affection from others to such a degree that it becomes detrimental and unhealthy. Unless someone is legitimately psychopathic, they will have some need within them to be loved and accepted by others. And this is perfectly normal. So how do we draw the line between a healthy and an unhealthy amount of codependency? Well, there are a few ways.

The first and most obvious is to take a step back and analyze how your relationships with people, substances, rituals, or anything else you can be dependent on is affecting your life. Do you receive benefits that come nowhere near close to the amount of energy you put in? Are you putting up with treatment that you would never give to someone else? Can you function and be content without your significant other?

If you answered yes to any of the above questions, it might be time to step back and take an objective look at how much you're relying on this person. If your codependency is truly a problem, it's likely that the issues you're having aren't only confined to your relationships. When things get out of control and your connection to your partner is threatened, you're likely to face emotional distress, including anger, frustration, sadness, despair, desperation, self-hatred, self-neglect, severe interpersonal agreements with both your partner and outsiders, and perhaps even suicidal thoughts.

Codependency can be harmful both to the codependent person and those in their lives for many reasons. The most obvious danger a codependent person faces is the potential for toxic relationships. When a codependent person enters a relationship, they automatically attach their personality, desires, and self-worth to their partner. This can lead to many problems, such as suppression of their true feelings, needs, or wants out of a fear of losing the relationship. It can also lead to them ignoring their own needs to keep their partner happy. These relationships don't allow the codependent individual to feel at ease when they're alone and make it very difficult for them to receive help because they always feel like they should be the ones helping.

Those with severe codependency probably have the criteria to be diagnosed with Dependent Personality Disorder, which is basically the only diagnosable form of codependency in the world of clinical psychology. It is a recognized personality disorder by all the major disease diagnostic manuals, including the Psychodynamic Diagnostic Manual (PDM), The Shedler-Westen Assessment Procedure (SWAP-200), the 10th Revision of the International Statistical Classification of Diseases and Related Health Problems (ICD), and the Diagnostic and Statistical Manual of Mental Disorders, Fifth Edition (DSM-5).

The DSM-5 states that an individual must have five of the following eight criteria to qualify for a diagnosis of Dependent Personality Disorder:

1. Has difficulty making everyday decisions without an excessive amount of advice and reassurance from others.

2. Needs others to assume responsibility for most major areas of their life.

3. Has difficulty expressing disagreement with others due to a fear of losing support or approval.

4. Has difficulty initiating projects or doing things on their own (due to a lack of self-confidence in judgment or abilities rather than a lack of motivation or energy).

5. Goes to excessive lengths to obtain nurturance and support from others to the point of volunteering in unpleasant activities.

6. Feels uncomfortable or helpless when alone because of exaggerated fears of being unable to care for themselves.

7. Urgently seeks another relationship as a source of care and support when a close relationship ends.

8. Is unrealistically preoccupied with fears of being left to take care of themselves.

Here, it is important to note that just because you don't meet the criteria for Dependent Personality Disorder doesn't mean that your problems should be disqualified in any sense. There are many different types of codependency; Dependent Personality Disorder describes only one of them. It doesn't mean that your codependency isn't an issue or causing problems in your life, or shouldn't be taken seriously. It absolutely should be.

THREE

What Causes Codependency?

C ODEPENDENCY IS OFTEN RECEIVED from others, either your parents or anyone else you were around growing up. This isn't to say that you can catch it like a cold, but it does mean that codependency rarely develops on its own. It's almost entirely a product of an individual's upbringing, which is something no child has ever been able to control. If you're confident that you have some form or degree of codependency, the very first step towards getting better is to understand that it isn't your fault that you're codependent. No one should have to endure the type of environment that results in someone developing codependent issues.

That's why this chapter is so important. You should understand why you're codependent so that you can begin to move past self-loathing and blaming yourself. In this section, we'll lay out in detail some of the circumstances and causes that lead to codependency. After reading this, if you do not see something that resembles or relates to your upbringing, that's okay. There are a million different ways codependency can develop. If you should take one thing away from this section, it's the understanding that codependency is an issue that has to do with personality, and there isn't a person in human history whose had control over their personality.

In short, codependency is caused by not receiving the right amount of love, attention, affection, approval, empathy, stability, kindness, understanding, openness, trust, or attentiveness in childhood. There are so many different ways your upbringing could've caused you not to feel the adequate amount of support you needed; it's impossible to list them all here. But we'll go through a rundown behind some general causes.

Like many different types of mental issues, codependency is almost always the result of an emotionally inadequate childhood. Children who have been neglected, abused, abandoned, or otherwise mistreated are the ones at risk for developing a problem with codependency. Also, it's been discovered that people who struggle with codependent behaviors often suffer from some underlying mental illness, whether this be a mood disorder such as Bipolar Disorder or Depression, Post-Traumatic Stress Disorder (PTSD), other types of personality disorders, or any other mental illness that can cause a person distress in their day to day life.

First, it's important to understand that all people (with the possible exception for psychopaths) have an instinctual innate need for acceptance, love, and support from the day they're born. This is largely a product of evolution. As you know, when humans were first developing, they were not the social animals they are today. There was a desire to be with others, but it wasn't as strong. When humans started traveling and taking on new tasks and environments, everything became harder and harder to do alone. As a result, people who didn't feel the need to be around others were much more likely to die, while individuals who lived together in communities were much more likely to survive. We are the product of that second type of group, and that's why we need approval, love, and affection so badly because when we don't have it, a primitive part of our brain remembers the dangers of being alone. Therefore, rejection fills us with a sense of dread, shame, and sadness.

When someone is mistreated for a long time from such a young age, the need for acceptance is poorly met. The strong, instinctual feeling of rejection and shame begins to permeate every part of their lives as they grow older without ever having felt the sort of love, approval, and affection they need. So, from a very young age, they look for ways to get it. This means that they have a constant fear of not being liked or accepted. They often don't make decisions on their own because they're afraid of angering someone. They have trouble voicing their needs, concerns, or wants because their childhood instilled in them that their opinions were unimportant, and only the caretaker's needs were ever given any attention.

From a very young age, codependent people were taught that they had to go to great lengths to receive the kind of love and approval many people take for granted. You'll find them trying to do everything they can for someone's approval. This can come in the form of paying their bills, taking care of their home, cooking their meals, taking care of their problems, and a lot more. Not only does this cost them a lot of energy along with disappointment, but it also causes them to put their own interests on the back burner and ignore them. They focus so much on improving this person's quality of life that their own life withers in the meantime.

Going to great lengths to take care of someone may also come from a need to "step up" if they have parents that don't take care of them either because they can't overcome their own problems, simply aren't willing, or both. In this case, it's easy to see how the caretaker attitude within a child who works hard to look after their siblings can be seen as a virtue, and be incredibly valuable as well as necessary within this environment. But this can also lead to problems later in life because they've been instilled that they have to do everything for everyone to keep them from falling apart.

An upbringing that taught you to be dependent on someone who caused you harm, physically or mentally, can also create codependency way down the line. When someone is trapped in a situation where the person they rely on is the same person who is abusing them, it can skew their sense of what is normal in the world. If they have little or no experience with any healthy type of dynamic, then often they don't realize exactly how toxic it is (though you may have an idea), and relationships in all parts of their life run the risk of following the same course. This is why children with abusive fathers often enter relationships with abusive partners. They become dependent on this sense of normalcy to find that acceptance they didn't have growing up.

Because their upbringing never taught them how far they should go to receive acceptance and approval from their caretakers, they will often go to extreme and unhealthy lengths to satisfy the person they need at the moment. This is a problem that has to do with establishing and following boundaries. For example, a woman might hate the fact that her boyfriend is cheating on her occasionally, but does nothing in the hopes that the opportunity he has to cheat will keep him happy with their relationship so he won't leave it.

One of the reasons codependents take on so much burden is that they were taught to be responsible for whatever problems they had during childhood. If someone is codependent and they see a problem someone close to them has, that problem is immediately their fault and their responsibility. They have an intense feeling of guilt, shame, self-hatred, and fear. These negative emotions give them almost an endless drive to satisfy the people they seek approval from.

Those who are dealing with codependency often don't have an understanding of how their upbringing affected them. One of the first things any therapist, counselor, or psychiatrist will ask a patient is what their childhood was like. Almost everyone, unless they suffered serious neglect or abuse, will say it was good or at least okay. Then they'll be asked about their parents, some of their most pleasant and least pleasant memories. And about three-quarters of them will answer with something that unquestionably counts as abuse, neglect, or dysfunctionality.

Most of us want to think of our parents as good people, and most of us are right. But it's important to know that your parents can be good, loving people and still do things that qualify as dysfunctional or worse. Maybe your father never talked but had an unpredictable, explosive temper, and you could never tell what would set it off. Maybe your mother would put problems she couldn't control onto your shoulders regularly and often cry over things you don't understand. Maybe you can't remember a single time in your life where you and your parents had a real connection or showed any kind of affection towards you. Just because they were there and supported you doesn't mean your childhood isn't a factor in the problems you're having now.

FOUR

Family Dysfunctions

T HE STRONGEST PREDICTOR OF codependency is having codependent parents. In the following sections, we'll look at the many common dysfunctional family dynamics. See if you find one that sounds familiar, and consider how the related mindset could affect your current relationships.

The Source of the Problem

In almost every dysfunctional family, there's someone in the center who is causing most of the problems. More often than not, this is a parent or someone else who assumes responsibility as the caretaker. Usually, this person's problems are said to come from only substance abuse, but it's more complicated than that. In fact, the family member who is the "source of the problem" can be dealing with any number of different issues at once, including but not limited to mental illness, brain injury, cancer, paralysis, anti-social behavior, abusive behavior, instability, or anything that can severely disrupt the family's normal life.

Whatever their issues are, it's always severe enough to become the axis around which the family rotates. Every aspect of the family, from where they live and go to school to when they eat and whom they interact with, is controlled by the needs or desires of this person. Their problem is often so overwhelming that every member of the family bases what they do and when they do it on this person's issue. This results in the needs, concerns, and interests of other family members to either be neglected, unmet, or outright ignored. There is nothing more important than this person and the problems they're facing.

Often, this person is not interested in or capable of recovery, and their needs and behaviors can dominate the family unit for years. Given that this person is either supposed to be the leader or at least a provider of the family, the other members are left to pick up the slack. They pick up the roles that this member was supposed to be filling. It's not uncommon in these types of situations for older siblings to take on the role of a parent. They're forced mature much more quickly than other children because the stakes are higher. If they don't do what needs to be done, then the whole family unit is at risk of falling apart. They do it not out of love or support for one another, but out of necessity. Something needs to get done, so someone steps up and does it. This can come in the form of providing food, education, transportation, or emotional support for the other members of the family.

Being that this member is the source of the problem, the only way the family can truly recover and reclaim their traditional roles is either by helping the member recover from their problem or removing them from the family unit completely.

The Glue

Given that the source of the problem is almost always a parent or someone who is supposed to be supporting the family, it often falls on the other parent or guardian to act as the sole provider. A sibling old enough to be in the workforce can also take on this role, but it's less common. This person is referred to as the Glue.

This role has the most obvious relation to codependency, but that's not to say that the Glue is always necessarily codependent. There are many reasons that do not involve codependency that would explain why a parent would become the Glue.

The first and most obvious is an obligation. With one provider out and the family still needing food, a place to stay, healthcare, and other needs, their sole purpose then becomes to keep the family afloat. This is not to say that they support the "source of the problem." They may be actively looking for a way to get them to recovery. However, it does mean that they decide to keep them within the family unit. This may be because they don't have the time or energy to remove them from the group, or they don't want to further injure their family by completely removing the source of the problem from their lives.

The Fixer

In the dysfunctional type of family in which everyone depends on a parent who has a problem that prevents them from supporting them, a common coping habit you'll find is that there is someone who tries to "fix" everything. This type is closely related to the Glue in that they inadvertently shield the source of the problem from the consequences of their actions. This results from the desire the Fixer has to save and protect the reputation of the family. To them, there's nothing more important than making the family appear normal, healthy, and functional to others.

This need to protect the family's reputation stems from a deep fear that the family will disintegrate if this facade fails. They fear the destruction of the family as they know it. They think that failing to protect the family's reputation often means losing a member and becoming separated from them. It can also mean losing the stability they experienced early on; so oftentimes, they trick themselves into believing that their current situation is acceptable because most people can't gather the willpower for such a role if they knew the actual bleakness of their family's situation.

In a vast majority of cases, this type is fulfilled by an older member of the family. Aunts, uncles, family, friends, or grandparents usually step into this role. However, the norm is to have this type fulfilled by either the oldest sibling or at least a sibling who has quite a few years over their brothers and sisters.

Like the Glue, the person who takes on and develops into this type will take on extra responsibilities and will often do anything within their power to keep the family together. Aside from the Glue, the Fixer is usually the most productive and useful member of the family. They can be very organized and responsible, even from a very young age. They often do well in school and are in good social standing. They also get along very well with their family and show affection and concern for everyone, including the source of the problem.

Yet, while on the outside, they may seem put together and content, they are almost always dealing with the invasive presence of negative emotions. Something that comes along with taking on this type is that someone has to view all of the family's needs and general wellbeing as a responsibility that is theirs alone. So when things get worse or problems arise (which will always happen), they blame themselves and are convinced that the problem is a result of a shortcoming on their end. This leads to guilt and self-loathing. And since their self-worth and happiness is directly dependent on the state of the family unit, they'll often work way more than is healthy in an attempt to improve their family's quality of life.

The Comedian

The Comedian is the first type in a dysfunctional family that does not try to fix or improve the family's quality of life. They tend not to take on extra responsibilities and draw a clear line between the family's problems and how much of it they're willing to deal with. As problems arise in the family unit, the Comedian will often do anything they can to get their minds off their troubles. They hide away from the family's issues and often refuse to recognize them.

As much as they don't want to deal with the problems in the family (which are often too complicated, overwhelming, or painful for them to handle), they are still affected by them. Like all the other types of dysfunctional family members, they develop a sense of resentment towards their current situation. Often, they feel tremendous amounts of frustration and depression when faced with their family's problems.

In an attempt to make themselves feel better, they'll look for ways to get away from or cope with the problems they face. This isn't unique among dysfunctional types, as there are others we'll discuss who develop coping mechanisms for dealing with painful emotions. But they are unique in that they try to relieve the distress of the family's situation by finding some kind of humor in it. By doing this, they trivialize their family's problems without realizing it, which can make them numb to how other members of the family will react. This often leads to their humor doing more harm than good.

The Daydreamer

The Daydreamer is the quietest type you'll find in dysfunctional families. This type stems from when a child is faced with a parent or caretaker who has a serious, incapacitating issue. Looking after someone who is supposed to be taking care of them is never a pleasant experience. The existence of the family unit as they know it is threatened, therefore, this family member experiences a significant amount of stress and anxiety. Many Daydreamers also don't have any support as they encounter these problems and try to cope with negative emotions. They often have no one to turn to or have trouble expressing their feelings to others because they don't feel close to anyone.

As a result, the Daydreamer has to teach themselves how to handle distressing emotions. When someone is placed into this sort of environment, it is common for them to withdraw as much as they can from participation or interaction with the family, especially if they are already prone to introversion. They see all the problems within their family and develop a significant fear of being the source of a problem themselves. Acting on this fear, they become quiet and make a substantial effort to stay out of people's way.

However, instead of helping them get rid of negative emotions, this behavior amplifies them. While they are eliminating a good amount of negative external stimuli, the effects of isolation develop a detrimental result. As they withdraw, the other members of the family pay less and less attention to them because they don't have the time to go out of their way for this one member. This makes the Daydreamer feel ignored and neglected, which severely damages their sense of self-worth.

As the Daydreamer falls deeper and deeper into isolation, they turn to other solutions to cure their negative emotions. A common way they attempt to do this is by developing a rich, vibrant fantasy world in which all their unsatisfied needs are met. These fantasies are often mirrored images of their current life. If someone's mother is helplessly addicted to alcohol, it's typical for them to create a world in their heads where their mother is sober.

The Fighter

The last type we'll cover in this chapter is the Fighter. Unlike the other types of ways people often cope with dysfunctional families, this type does not try to avoid or fix the family's problems. Instead, they embrace it head-on. They are filled with frustration and depression just like the other coping types, but they use these negative emotions as fuel to express just how troubled and unhappy they feel.

The Fighter will often resist all different kinds of authority. This can be a subconscious effort to create problems outside of the family to distract themselves from the issues within. Their anger makes them very prone to causing trouble and getting into fights. Often, they will not follow orders and will go out of their way to break the rules.

The only way to help a Fighter is to remove the source of the family's problem because that's what's causing their frustration, depression, emptiness, and behavior. Since they're faced with circumstances that hurt them and have no power to change it, they feel mistreated, and therefore, don't have to obey the same rules others do. Another factor that drives the Fighter is the lack of control they've had over their lives. When they choose to act out, from their perspective, it puts them in control of their lives. Often, this need to have some control and structure outweighs the consequences of what they have to do to get it.

All the Fighter ever does is to try and take away their feelings of depression and lack of control. Acting out only brings them temporary relief of their distress, but it's often the only way they know how to make themselves feel better, which puts them at risk for developing substance abuse issues later.

Making positive changes

If any of these roles outlined looks familiar, understand that you can change these situations. For many people, the reason that they carry these dysfunctional roles into adulthood, along with all the codependent tendencies that come along with it, is that they are still subconsciously waiting for their parents to give them permission to change.

However, it would help if you recognized that real change begins with you. To get started, you need to make a list of difficult or painful memories from your childhood. Next to each item on your list, you need to write down an alternate behavior or belief you would like to experience instead. Then, organize your list based on which issues you think will be the easiest to implement.

From there, make a conscious effort to complete the first change on your list. Even if it's supposed to be the easiest item on your list, it might be a bit challenging to change because you are forming a new habit at the same time. But if you power through, you'll find it easier to make it through the rest of your list. Keep this up, and before you know it, you'll be free and ready to move forward with a little less baggage.

FIVE

Addiction and Codependency

S OME PEOPLE CALL CODEPENDENCY itself a "relationship" or "love addiction." But this limits the concept of codependency within the confines of a relationship. In reality, codependency also includes any unhealthy obsession or dependence someone has to a particular object, such as a drug. The reasons behind interpersonal codependency and substance codependency are similar, if not identical. In both cases, a person's self-worth, interests, needs, and actions are centered around something other than themselves. In this chapter, we'll lay out what an individual who is dependent on drugs looks like, and then we'll look at codependency and substance abuse in the framework of a relationship or family.

Addiction and Codependency Go Hand in Hand

The causes of addiction and codependency are very similar. Both stem from a constant need to have something not only to function but also to feel happy. A person is far more susceptible to addiction when they are not satisfied with either themselves or their life. A person becomes codependent both because they aren't content with who they are as a person and because their life seems unbearable without someone else.

A relationship in which one person is codependent to an unhealthy degree usually doesn't last very long, but while it lasts, the codependent individual can feel incredible amounts of relief, satisfaction, joy, and love. If this is their current state, their risk of addiction is pretty low. But when the relationship ends and that void they were using the other person to fill is empty again, their chances of addiction increases. The dynamic behind codependence fosters addiction. A codependent person is used to relying on something else to feel content with themselves and their lives, and they will often turn to anything that will work to end the emotional pain and emptiness they feel. Codependents have a higher risk of addiction, but this is not a direct result of their codependency. Instead, it's a result of the emotional pain they feel.

But codependents are much more likely to exacerbate someone else's substance abuse problem than they are to develop one themselves. This was first identified by the minds behind Alcoholics Anonymous, who studied the nature of alcoholism at length. They found that not all of an addict's problems were the result of their upbringing or current behavior. Instead, the people in the addict's life had the potential to lay a major roadblock on the addict's path to recovery.

This is a result of the basic nature of codependency. The majority of the time, a codependent person will not enter a relationship with a stable, well-put-together, independent individual. Instead, they'll look for partners that are struggling with problems, such as emotions, finance, health, or substance abuse. This is because codependents have a burning desire to be needed and for someone to depend on them for something important. This isn't to say that codependents prey on their partners — that's not true at all. They often enter these types of relationships with honest and intense feelings of love, empathy, and acceptance. While this is done in the hope that they'll receive the same amount of care back, it isn't done consciously. They will often do everything in their power to help their partner with their struggles.

Another reason codependents often enter relationships with people who struggle with substance abuse is that they are familiar with the terrain. If you'll recall, one of the first mainstream books to popularize the concept of codependency was Adult Children of Alcoholics, which examined the behaviors many children with alcoholic parents had in their adult lives. If someone grew up with a caretaker who had problems with substance abuse and never experienced a healthy upbringing, then having a partner with such issues will be their idea of a "normal" relationship. Furthermore, codependent individuals will often go to such lengths because they feel as though, with all the experience they had with addiction in their upbringing, they know exactly what to do and how to help.

Since individuals who struggle with substance abuse issues suffer a lot, the codependent person can be a sort of "sponge" that can soak up all the problems, pain, and suffering. The problem here is that codependent people think that making their partner's life easier is the same as helping them. But it isn't. There is a big difference between helping someone and taking care of someone, and the dangers of the latter will be discussed in this next section.

Enabling an Addiction

Despite having all the goodwill in the world, codependent individuals rarely succeed in helping their partners with substance abuse. In fact, they are much more likely to make the situation worse by prolonging it and shielding their significant other from the consequences of addiction. I say significant other here only because the most common type of person to enable an addict's addiction is their spouse, but anyone close to the addict can enable their addiction, whether it be a parent, sibling, or friend.

To understand why codependent people so often enable their spouse's addiction, we first need to understand two things: the over-helpfulness of codependency and the stages of addiction.

Codependents will do whatever it takes to keep their partners happy. As a result, they avoid putting anything that may be unpleasant on their partner's shoulders. They think that, if their partner is unhappy, then they run the risk of potentially ending the relationship, and that's the last thing they want. Their only focus is to keep their partner happy, and this is where problems develop.

An addiction starts slow. Someone may use a substance occasionally without issue for years before they develop a problem. This usually happens when they're unhappy with some other aspect of their life, and so will turn more and more to substances to mask the pain. An illusory aspect of addiction that most addicts face is the inability to see the negative impact substance abuse is having on their lives and those around them. This is because most addicts don't spiral fast; they spiral slow. So when something terrible happens, they label it as just one unfortunate event, causing them to ignore the fact that they've lost a lot.

It takes a lot to get an addict to quit. Almost no addicts quit without reason. As their addiction takes over their lives more and more, the cost of their substance abuse grows. Eventually, the damage of their addiction will reach a point where it's evident that it's no longer worth it. They've lost or stand to lose so much that suddenly, they find the willpower to quit. This is what they call "rock bottom," which is a wake-up call to get their act together because things couldn't possibly get any worse than they currently are.

The problem with a codependent "taking care" of an addict is that they don't allow them to reach rock bottom. They offer them a safe, accepting, and stable environment to continue their addiction. As long as the addict has this support, it's much harder for them to find the willpower to quit.

This is what has become known as "enabling an addiction." It begins with good intentions but can have disastrous consequences.

There are many different things a codependent person may do to support their partner or protect them from the consequences of their actions. Some are rather small and inane, but others are much more harmful to both of them in the long run. Some of the things we often see, probably more than anything else in relationships that enable addictions, is the codependent person supplying financial support to help fund their partner's habit. We also see them lying to friends, family, bosses, or even the police. Often, they will take on all of the responsibilities in their relationship (at least as much as they can). This includes doing all the work around the house, taking care of the kids, paying the mortgage, rent, or other bills, cooking for them, and making them as comfortable as possible. If things get so serious that law enforcement gets involved, codependents are often more than willing to lie for them, provide them with an alibi, support them as a witness, or post bail to get them out of jail.

While this is often a very painful experience for the addict and their partner, the codependent person is usually not willing or even open to change without intervention. Even if everyone else in the family is suffering and their lives are falling apart, the codependent person feels an immense sense of satisfaction and joy throughout much of it. Every time their partner presents them with some other responsibility they can't handle, they pick it up without question or resentment. Although this kind of behavior can result in extreme overwhelm, codependents will look for even more responsibilities to take on. To us, this dynamic is obviously toxic, unhealthy, and unsustainable; but to the codependent person, they are just proving their worth. They are not only needed, but the relationship would fall apart without them. They are the single piece of glue holding it all together.

Sadly, while the codependent person will take on as much as they can to help their partner, it often doesn't pay off the way they think it will. When they do so much for someone else, they expect something in return that has an equal or at least a similar level of effort and love. But this doesn't happen. They don't get the acceptance or love they need. So they just try harder, and harder, and harder. If they could try and make it work forever, they would. But it always comes apart somehow.

In this type of situation, one of the major problems is that codependent people can't tell the difference between loving someone and taking care of someone. In their minds, the concept that you can love and support someone while letting them do things on their own and even suffer is inconceivable. They think that, if they don't show their love and worth at every single opportunity, then their partner will have no reason to stay with them. This is a result of their upbringing, where they had to do extraordinary things to receive the love and acceptance they should've received.

It is a mature thing to know when to walk away. Codependents don't have that. Sometimes, codependent people can, over time, identify their problems in some way and help themselves out of these types of situations; but often, especially with serious cases of codependency, it requires either some other person to intervene or for something dramatic to occur. Again, this codependent behavior is their baseline; it's normal for them. It has worked for them in the past, so they fully expect it will work again. But a codependent person can also be the biggest obstacle blocking an addict from recovery and sobriety. This is only one of the problematic dynamics codependent people find themselves in.

Vices and Codependency

The world we live in today has an inconsistent view of vices. Some of them, such as alcohol, tobacco, gambling, or sex, are perfectly acceptable by vast amounts of people. Other ones, however, such as illicit drugs and dangerous activities, are not. Nevertheless, even vices that are accepted by society can lead to a range of serious issues. You can drink yourself to the point of liver failure by the time you're in your thirties, give yourself cancer by chain-smoking cigarettes, and lose all your money by gambling.

When someone in a relationship is faced with any of the vices this society has deemed to be acceptable, it can be hard for them to decide which ones are acceptable and which ones are problematic. If you have a feeling that your partner's gambling habits might be a problem, it is likely that you'll face an uphill battle in getting them to control it since it's legal and may be accepted among your community.

In the same way, you can become complicit and supportive of something your partner is doing that causes a lot of damage to their life. If you try to seek support from someone else and it turns out that they don't see your partner's gambling as a problem the same way you do, it can be difficult to avoid enabling it.

This is why it's important to view your relationship within a vacuum. Just because something is socially acceptable and doesn't cause distress to the families of those who partake in it doesn't mean that it's healthy and acceptable behavior. The only two things you should take into account are your own emotions and feelings, as well as the current state and projection of your life.

Six

Stages of a Codependent Relationship

U NLIKE OTHER MENTAL HEALTH problems, codependency requires something outside of the affected individual to influence them. You can be prone to codependency and have nothing that you're unhealthily attached to at the moment, but you cannot be actively codependent without being attached to a person, substance, or object to an unhealthy degree. Codependence on something else gets worse over time. In this chapter, we'll cover the different stages of codependent relationships, how they develop, and the consequences of each of them.

The Romantic Stage

Codependent people have the tendency to jump head-first from one relationship to another. As soon as a person prone to codependency enters a relationship, their partner already plays a huge role in their lives. This is called the Romantic Stage of codependency, and it's the most enjoyable stage. But it's hard to tell whether it's just a powerful dose of love between the two couples or if it's the beginning stages of codependency.

Some of us have experienced what's known as "love at first sight," the process where you're in love (or at least very infatuated) with your partner. One day we're going about our lives minding our own business when suddenly we meet someone and bam — we're in love. There's something there that draws us to them, makes us think about them from the time we wake up until we go to bed. We seldom know what it is, but we feel it there, and that's enough. Suddenly, our whole world revolves around this person. They are our joy and sorrow. There's no clear line between this kind of intense love and codependency. The only real way to differentiate between the two is to analyze your own feelings. Are you attached to this person because you love everything about them? Or is it because you're no longer alone? Do you rely a great amount on their love and attention for your own self-worth?

We should also clarify here that codependency is not exclusive to romantic relationships. Codependence can sneak its way into the relationships we have with friends, mentors, or anyone else that support us. However, the majority of codependent relationships are between significant others. If someone is prone to codependency, then every relationship in their life is susceptible to it.

Love, infatuation, and the Romantic Stage of codependency are three emotional states found in new relationships, and it's hard to tell one apart from the other. Nevertheless, here are some of the things you'll find in the early stage of a codependent relationship.

One aspect of early codependency that can be identified rather easily is the type of person you're with. As we've discussed in the last chapter, people who are prone to codependency automatically search for partners that could be called "projects." These people usually have their share of problems and don't function well on their own. They have a lot of needs, and there's plenty of room for their codependent partner (who has a ton of energy when it comes to taking care of others and proving their worth) to improve their lives and situation. So, if someone who is doing well begins dating a person who has problems, it's time to look for more signs of codependency.

Another good way to identify the early stages of code-pendency in a relationship is looking to see whether or not a partner is neglecting other parts of their lives and shifting the balance of things. This mostly comes in the form of neglecting other relationships because there's little to nothing else that the codependent person would rather do than be around their partner. If someone goes from spending a good amount of time with their friends to never seeing them at all, a proneness to codependency might be the culprit.

The Realist Stage

This stage is where the real problems that come with dependency are revealed. The Romantic stage, where both the codependent person and their partner "fell in love" and everything seemed equal, and they felt adequate, accepted, and loved, usually ends much faster than expected, and it often happens quickly and all at once. In the course of a day, the codependent person goes from being fulfilled, happy, and satisfied to worried, distressed, and noticeably dependent.

This stage begins when the codependent person stops feeling secure in the relationship. This can occur due to several reasons. The most common being their partner showing some level of independence. This is never done on purpose, but either way, the codependent person interprets it as "I don't need you," which terrifies them. It also happens when their partner doesn't live up to giving the same amount of love or affection they gave in the first stage. Here, the codependent person feels like they're losing their partner and that frightens them. As a result, they move towards more radical codependent behaviors.

They start looking for more and more things they can do for their partner to prove their worth. It serves as a way for them to show their partner how much they love them and how valuable they are. While this is being done, they're hoping that their actions will result in two things: 1) their partner staying with them, and 2) their partner showing the same amount of love and effort back.

It isn't a conscious decision, but by doing these things, the codependent person is trying to gain control. As they do more and more for their partner, their partner will become more dependent on them — relying on them to cook, sort out the finances, keep the home running, and much else. This way, if their partner does want to end the relationship, they'll have to go without all these perks.

While a codependent person will almost certainly do some form of the above in the second stage, it won't help the one thing that really drove them to do it — the emotional pain they're in. While it may evoke some extra affection at first from their partner, they'll soon become desensitized to it and just view it as normal. After a while, they might not show any appreciation at all.

This results in a stressful period for the codependent individual. They start to feel guilty at the idea that they're not enough for their partner or making them happy. As they do more to establish their importance and receive love and affection, they will get nothing in return. This causes them to feel powerless in doing everything to change the course of the relationship and relieve them of their distress.

But instead of seeking outside support, they will double down on their effort. The end of this stage is where a codependent person will become overbearing and even controlling, further straining the relationship with their partner. They will further neglect their other relationships and responsibilities as their codependence takes up more of their time. It's a nasty slope because they become isolated and unhappy as it goes on, and the only thing they can think of is to try and do something else for their partner.

Towards the end of the Realist Stage, they begin taking the blame for things they didn't do in hopes to win over some extra affection from their partner. They're willing to put up with toxic behaviors, which can be as serious as substance abuse or violence.

The Painful Stage

The painful stage ends in one of two ways: either the relationship will endure before recovery can begin, or both partners will be stuck in the relationship until it crashes and burns.

Examining this stage can show us just how dangerous unchecked codependency can be. Here, the relationship has become downright toxic. Both the codependent person and their partner have become so stubborn that recovery while saving the relationship is hopeless. The consequences of codependency have gone to the point where the detriment on both people's lives is clearly visible.

The Painful Stage of a codependent relationship is just that — painful. Not a pretty sight. Whatever problems or responsibilities the codependent person was shielding their partner from becomes severe. If their partner were struggling with substance abuse, they would become completely and helplessly addicted. They need it every day. They use it every day. They need it to function. Often, their partner is unemployed at this point and rarely capable of taking on any meaningful responsibilities.

Every aspect of the couple's life has been affected. Usually, only the codependent person is employed, and it's not uncommon to see relationships where the couple has lost their original home or place of residence due to financial restraints. They've often been forced to move somewhere much cheaper, back in with their parents or other relatives, or possibly even homeless.

The scope of both partner's day to day lives has narrowed dramatically. They've neglected almost every other relationship they have and usually do not spend any significant amount of time with anyone but each other. Both partners are under a tremendous amount of stress, which can sometimes cause at least one of them to develop a major health problem. Their self-worth has been severely damaged. The codependent person feels as if they've failed to take care of their partner. They are often quite unsatisfied with the relationship and desperately crave love and affection. Their partner, on the other hand, usually doesn't make any meaningful progress towards solving their problems. They either feel useless and pathetic or have simply stayed in the relationship for the support their partner gives them rather than any genuine interest to be there.

At his point, the codependent person will have great anxiety and depression. They don't see a way out; yet, unless there's some form of outside intervention or an epiphany about their codependency, they don't stop the behaviors that got them there in the first place. As a result, all the care-taking they were doing changes from a way to make their partner value and love them to more of a set of obsessive rituals that they convince themselves they have to do to keep the relationship together. This can mean doing the same things multiple times a day, cleaning things that don't need to be cleaned, taking care of things that don't need to be taken care of, going on radical diets, exercising to an unhealthy degree, and other types of obsessive-compulsive disorders.

The Painful Stage of codependency also puts the codependent person at risk for developing substance abuse issues themselves. Their mental state can get to the point where they cannot hold down a job or function away from their partner. We've also seen people in the last stages of a codependent relationship develop severe eating disorders. Usually, they starve themselves or purge as an attempt to take back some form of control in their lives.

The Painful Stage of codependency can last years, possibly until the end of the couple's lives. In this stage, it's very unlikely that they'll break up without some sort of outside intervention. Both people have become so dependent on one another that life apart is inconceivable. It would be like starting over in a different world, especially if they've been together for years.

A Short message from the Author:

Hey, are you enjoying the Codependent Cure? I'd love to hear your thoughts!

Many readers do not know how hard reviews are to come by, and how much they help an author.

I would be incredibly grateful if you could take just 60 seconds to write a brief review on Amazon, even if it's just a few words!

>> To leave a brief review, please visit <u>www.TitleRatings</u> <u>.com/Codependent</u> or **scan the QR code above**

Thank you for taking the time to share your thoughts!

Your review will genuinely make a difference for me and help me gain exposure for my work.

SEVEN

Are You Codependent?

ALTHOUGH AN UPBRINGING THAT wasn't sufficiently loving, healthy, and supportive can certainly cause someone to become prone to codependency, which is found in a majority of codependent individuals, they can still be codependent when these factors are present. People's issues should never be disqualified because of circumstances they can't control. There are thousands of different variables they can experience in their life that can cause some form of codependency to develop. Financial stress, an injury, or entering a toxic relationship can all lead to codependent behavior. Also, being codependent doesn't mean that you lack emotional intelligence, though this can sometimes be a factor.

Anyone can be prone to codependency. Furthermore, although codependency was originally defined as being inseparable from a family unit with an alcoholic individual at its center, it has since come to be understood as some thing that can affect anyone at any point in their life. Being codependent can simply mean displaying codependent behaviors among your social circle, family, relationships, or substance use. It can also describe the dynamics of a relationship you're in at the moment.

The purpose of this section is to lay out a clear guide to determine whether or not you are displaying codependent behavior or in a codependent relationship. This section is not meant to diagnose anyone with anything; it's only here to help you understand the signs of codependency, as well as what qualifies as abnormally codependent behavior.

The People Pleaser

One of the most visible and damaging aspects of codependent behavior is the need codependent individuals feel to keep the people in their life happy. This occurs for a few reasons.

First, codependent individuals have a weak or damaged sense of self; this is possibly due to an unsupportive upbringing or a traumatic experience in adulthood. They have a problem seeing themselves as a person who exists on their own and not in relation to anyone else. The image a codependent person has of themselves is based on the opinions of those around them. For them, it's either hard or impossible to take an objective look at themselves and do a factual inventory of their strengths and weaknesses. So in order for the codependent person to have a positive image or idea of themselves, they must receive constant affirmation of their worth and virtue from someone else. This leads to two problems. One, many relationships don't offer this kind of constant reassurance to either party, so the other person often feels pressured and overwhelmed by the codependent person's need for approval. Two, this kind of affirmation from one or two people is often not nearly enough for a codependent person to be satisfied and think highly of themselves — they need approval from everyone they have a meaningful relationship with.

Second, codependents have not only a severe sense of abandonment but also a deep-rooted fear of being alone. They feel an extraordinary amount of positive emotions when someone else shows them love and affection. This display is so significant that they quickly become reliant on it to keep them happy. So dependency starts very early on. The reason that they are pleased when someone else shows them love and kindness is that codependent individuals are often unable to show that kind of treatment to themselves. For whatever reason, they never learned how to love themselves. Because this internal emotional balance is either severely or entirely lacking, they are forced to rely on others for it. As a result, their biggest fear is going into a relationship only to have it end (which most relationships do). They often can't articulate it, but they fear being alone. Their weak sense of self leads to a chronic feeling of emptiness when no outside affirmation is present. So codependents will often turn to anything they can to avoid being alone or feeling abandoned.

However, it's completely normal to want to keep those around you happy. Humans have an innate desire to take care of our own, and there's nothing unhealthy about it. So how does someone know when their need to keep others happy is problematic? Well, the answer requires a lot of soul-searching and self-reflection. But here are a few useful questions you can ask yourself.

"Do you expect something in return when you do something for someone?"

It's always good to give, but you should give for the right reasons. The concept behind this question is that someone will treat a person in the same way that that person treats them. If a codependent person feels starved for affection, their strategy is to shower their partner with kindness and passion in hopes of receiving the same level of support in return. Yet, while someone will react positively to being treated this way, it rarely ever results in them returning the same amount of affection. When a codependent tries this and doesn't receive the love they need, it can damage their self-worth and cause resentment. There is absolutely nothing wrong with doing this as long as you don't expect anything in return. If you're going to support someone in this manner, accept them as they are, not as the source of affection you may want them to be.

"Does your self-esteem fluctuate radically after good or bad interactions with other people?"

To the codependent person, there's nothing that can make them feel worse than discovering that someone is unhappy with them. At the same time, nothing makes them feel better than discovering that someone thinks highly of them. It's natural to feel emotions after positive or negative interactions, but it is neither normal nor healthy for someone to feel intense emotions after these situations.

A positive interaction with a non-codependent person will be pleasant and perhaps serve as a little mood boost for the next few hours. However, a positive interaction with a codependent person will often be the best thing that's happened to them all week. It will fill them with confidence and a powerful sense of well-being, and they'll likely think about that single interaction for a long time, sometimes years after it happened.

A negative interaction with a non-codependent person will be unpleasant and uncomfortable, and may make them question some of the choices they made as they analyze what led to the conflict throughout the day. However, a negative interaction with a codependent person can be emotionally catastrophic. They will feel huge waves of shame, anxiety, and depression as the interaction unfolds. They will often be very apologetic and attempt to reconcile the conflict as soon as possible. Afterward, they may feel a great sense of urgency to change and better themselves since they might think that the conflict was completely their fault and a sign that there's something wrong with them.

Relying on Someone

Opposite to "people-pleasing," and yet still a toxic aspect of codependency, is depending a great deal on other people for financial, emotional, or any other kind of support. This comes about for a few reasons. Codependents don't usually rely on someone because they consciously consider themselves incapable of independence. Instead, they rely on others because they experience unpleasant emotions when they're off by themselves without emotional support. They probably couldn't articulate it if you asked them to, but they are chronically unhappy when they're alone.

An unhealthy dependence can form between the codependent individual and anyone they have a relationship with, whether it'd be a parent, spouse, sibling, friend, therapist, or anyone else who supports them. Now it is natural to have to turn to others in times of need. Someone struggling with a health problem or any other debilitating issue will not be codependent in a real sense if they have difficulty taking care of themselves. For someone to be truly codependent, they need to have the capability of taking care of themselves. If someone still relies on someone else when they are fully capable of being independent, then we can start considering codependency.

It can sometimes be challenging to determine whether or not you are overly reliant on another person. When someone is in an intimate relationship with someone else, there is a natural, healthy level of dependence that develops between the two. So, again, we'll offer up a few basic questions you can ask yourself to determine whether or not you have an unhealthy amount of dependence.

"Is there an uneven amount of dependency in the dynamic of the relationship?"

In codependent relationships, we sometimes see one person relying more heavily on their partner for emotional support than their partner does. Codependents will often lean completely on their spouse to provide emotional support and happiness. In these cases, if their partner doesn't rely on them in the same sense, the codependent will find themselves feeling a certain amount of imbalance in the relationship. They often get the sense that they are more into their spouse than their spouse is into them.

"Do you feel intensely distressed when the two of you are apart for any period?"

An aspect of a codependent person is that they can spend the entire day with their partner, have a great time, do everything together, and then go home feeling horrible. Although nothing terrible happened, they feel unloved, and their self-worth is at a low point. This is because they were given affirmations of their value all day long, but as soon as they are separated from their partner, those affirmations go away, as does the contentedness and joy that they were feeling. It's natural to miss someone you love, but the littlest, shortest time apart shouldn't evoke powerful sensations of depression and anxiety.

"Are other aspects of your life dependent on this person?"

Codependents not only need affirmation in the relationship, but they also need it for everything they do on a daily basis. If they have a job, they need to hear that they're good at it and are valued as an employee. If they have a child, they need to hear that they're a good, loving parent. If they're creating a piece of art, they need to hear that it's good and worthwhile. In codependent relationships, the codependent seeks (without meaning to) the affirmations of all of these things from their partner.

Submissiveness

Another distinct aspect of codependency is the inability of the codependent person to assert themselves. They often go along with whatever the other person wants, and there are a few reasons for this.

Naturally, asserting yourself usually includes opposing the will or authority of someone else. In these types of situations, it's natural and common for conflicts to arise. Moreover, conflicts can cause those involved to feel frustration and many other types of negative emotions towards the other person. In short, when you assert yourself, you are running the risk of making the other person unhappy with you. As we've already established, codependents place a great deal of importance on what other people think of them. A conflict could easily bring about loads of emotional pain to them if things get heated. As a result, most codependents view asserting themselves as too big of a risk to take.

Another reason that codependents have trouble with assertion has to do with their weak sense of self. When your personality is tied so closely to that of another person, it can be hard to determine what you want or how you really feel about something. Codependents can be easily won over to something they may oppose as an individual because they are so unsure of the authority and virtue of their own opinion.

If someone is in a codependent relationship, chances are that there will be some amount of submission. Codependents will often make little or no effort to make their voice heard. If they do, it's usually as passive and non-threatening as they can make it. Even when they do assert themselves, their willpower is quickly overcome when faced with any amount of pushback from the other person. This isn't the same as making compromises. All relationships need compromises from both sides to be healthy and sustainable. But it is generally easy to tell whether or not you're being diplomatic or submissive. Here are a few questions to help you do that.

"How frequently do you and your partner have conflicts?

Do you go to great lengths to avoid conflicts?

Lastly, when was the last time you won an argument with your spouse?"

It's expected for couples to argue. When two people spend large amounts of time together, differences in their personality will clash and cause conflict. In the same way that too many fights are an issue, having too few conflicts can be somewhat problematic. "Never arguing" doesn't usually mean that a couple is so in tune with each other that they hardly ever have conflicts. Instead, it most likely means that one of them is hiding their true feelings to keep the other one happy.

"Do you find yourself doing a lot of things you don't like or resent in the course of your relationship?"

Different people like different things. Your partner might not like John Carpenter movies as much as you do, but they'll still sit down and watch one with you from time to time. However, if you find yourself doing things you don't enjoy so often that you've begun to dread them, take a moment and ask why you let yourself be subjected to these activities. It may be that the possibility of your spouse reacting negatively if you don't do what they want to do is the driving force behind this behavior. Your relationship probably has some level of codependency or another similar type of dysfunction

Unpleasant Emotions

One thing that always, without fail, comes with codependency is unpleasant emotions. All codependent behavior is driven by the need to escape from negative emotions. These can be emptiness, depression, anxiety, frustration, feelings of neglect, and any other type of emotion that causes distress.

Despite their best efforts, they never escape these emotions through further codependent behavior. While codependents may think that their relationship is fulfilling and healthy in a rational sense, they still can't shake the invasive thoughts and emotions that something isn't right, things are about to go wrong, or they're secretly not enough.

While it's easy for a person in a healthy mental state to identify the unpleasant emotions codependent people experience as unhealthy and problematic, it's often much harder for codependents to recognize them. This is because codependency and the emotions that come with it are deeply rooted. Likely, these sorts of feelings have been present ever since the individual had any sense of emotional intelligence or self-awareness. In other words, they've never known anything else. The daily presence of these negative emotions is normal to them.

Something that people with poor upbringings are surprised to realize when they start seeking mental health care is that it isn't normal to feel negative emotions for most of their waking hours. In an evolutionary framework, emotions serve as a signal that something is wrong. Usually, when someone went from feeling happy to depressed, it was a sign that something in their life wasn't sufficiently meeting their needs. The negative emotions served as an alarm bell which would sound when something about their lives needed to change, usually due to reasons outside of their control.

We've lost this signal in the modern world. Our society has become more complex than humans who lived only a few centuries ago could possibly imagine. In the process, the very biological signals our body provided us with as a form of checks and balances was confounded, and now the presence of negative emotions could mean many different things.

This isn't to say that you are codependent if you experience negative emotions in a relationship, but it does mean something is wrong, whether that is a mental illness, unfulfilling life, poor nutrition, sedentary lifestyle, or several other things.

So how do we identify someone's negative emotions as a sign of codependency? Well, there's a simple question you can ask yourself:

"Are you feeling negative emotions in the areas of life that relate to codependency?"

Codependency is often overwhelming. If you are codependent, the odds are that you will feel bad in most of the different areas associated with codependency. To review, these areas include: being away from your spouse for an extended amount of time, basing your self-worth on other people's opinions, experiencing self-hatred after small conflicts, sacrificing your own needs and interests to meet those of someone else, trying to take care of other people more than you take care of yourself, and relying on someone else to make you feel important.

EIGHT

The Art of Detachment

T HERE'S A GOOD CHANCE that at this point, you're certain that you might be in a codependent relationship. Depending on how long you've been together, the problems you and your partner are facing, and what stage of codependency you're in at the moment, you could be under a tremendous amount of stress.

By picking up this book and committing to reading it, hopefully you've gotten a greater understanding of your issues than any other one text has ever given you. You can now identify problematic and unhealthy behaviors in your relationship, which is the very first step towards improving your relationship and your life.

While this book can help codependent individuals dramatically, it is not a magical solution to your problems. To truly recover from codependency, you need the willpower and a strong desire to change. This chapter will provide you with some strategies to make your road to recovery as easy as possible.

Identifying a Codependent Relationship

Before you do anything, you should make sure that codependency is the issues you are facing within your relationship. There are a few different ways you can determine this.

First of all, you can take a long, in-depth look at the dynamics between you and your partner. What is the current state of your lives and are you satisfied with it? It will help if you keep track of everything you do for the relationship, and compare it with how much your partner does in return. It's natural for one partner to do a little more than the other, but a sure sign of codependent relationships is a radical disparity between how much you do and how much your partner does.

It can be confusing to realize that you do so much more than your partner because, if you're codependent, there's a good chance that you take great pleasure in doing much more than what is asked for you. Even if you don't take pleasure in it at this point, you may still feel a strong obligation to go above and beyond what your partner does. Identifying the imbalance in the effort that you and your partner put in is one of the most important things to know before you begin recovery. It can also be a problem when you find your partner doing too many things for you. Conversely, your partner coming to rely too much on you for things they should be doing themselves may also suggest codependency.

Another way you can identify codependency is by analyzing how well you get along with your partner when they're either upset with you or not around. As we've discussed before, codependent people often have a difficult time being away from someone they're close to.

Codependency and Narcissism

When it comes to relationships, codependency and narcissism are very closely related. Not in the sense that a codependent person is also prone to narcissism (the opposite is true in fact), but in the sense that codependent people are attracted to narcissists and vice versa.

Interestingly, narcissist and codependents are two sides of the same coin. They both come out of the same sorts of environments. When someone is deprived of love and affection from an early age, it can go one of two ways:

1) they can become obsessed with seeking the affection of others, or 2) see themselves as a superior outsider who doesn't need to conform to social norms, and can exploit and dominate others because they're so much better.

To explain the relationship between codependency and narcissism, we need to understand what a narcissist is. A narcissist is someone who puts their well-being and interests over those of others. They often have no problem taking advantage of other people by using them to get what they want. They think of themselves as a superior person, someone who is second to no one regarding ability, physical attractiveness, and intelligence.

The relationship between a codependent person and a narcissist can be especially toxic. This is because one behavioral abnormality compliments the other in this unique type of bond. At the same time, as the codependent turns to do everything they possibly can to satisfy the narcissist (who are often very troubled by their own issues caused by their self-serving behavior), the narcissist attempts to manipulate the codependent into doing things for them that they should be doing themselves. This can come in many different forms, such as the codependent taking on a narcissist's debt, providing the things necessary for them to do whatever they want, or taking responsibility away from them.

In short, the narcissist benefits greatly from the relationship while the codependent suffers. What's even more troubling about relationships between codependents and narcissists is that they are much more difficult to get out of than other types of relationships codependents may find themselves in. Even non-codependent people who find themselves in a relationship with a narcissist often face trouble when they decide to leave. This occurs for two reasons. First, the narcissist will likely be very dependent on their partner by the time their partner tries to leave the relationship. And second, narcissists are very good at manipulation, and there are a few different ways they go about messing with their partner's heads.

One of the main ways they do this is called Gaslighting. Gaslighting is a subtle form of manipulation that is done by making the victim question their own senses, memory, or judgment. It's usually done in disagreements about what the narcissist did wrong. When blamed for something, they will skillfully disagree with what happened and find some way to put the blame on their partner. Some narcissists are so skillful and trained in this form of manipulation that it's often very difficult for the other person to really know for sure what exactly happened and who is at fault.

It is also tricky for codependent people to remove themselves from relationships with narcissists because, when they're finally gaining a new perspective on life, setting boundaries, and examining their relationships with others, the narcissist remains unchanged and is often impermeable to shifting their behavior. As the codependent gets better, the narcissist only gets worse. And this leaves the codependent to deal with the fact that they've been in a relationship with someone who is extremely selfish, callous, and apathetic.

Handling the Relationship

If you find yourself in a codependent relationship, there are a few things you can do to smooth things over and begin the process of healing and change.

The first and perhaps most important step you should take when you find yourself in a codependent relationship is realizing that you are at least partially responsible for creating the codependent dynamic between you and your partner. This isn't to say that you're at fault for being prone to codependent behavior. All this means is that a codependent relationship requires two people. No one is at fault, and no one should feel bad or guilty. However, you are both responsible for creating the codependent relationship.

The next step is to open a line of communication about it with your partner. This is rarely a pleasant experience. Often your partner will show resistance to what you are proposing in some way (if both of you are truly codependent), which can be done by them denying their past behavior or arguing with you as to what exactly counts as codependency. Although this can be a very different conversation to have, it's a line of communication that needs to be opened between the two of you.

Once you and your partner are on the same page about your issues, you should start looking for more information about codependency. As you come to understand it better, make sure you have an open line of communication with your partner. This will help both of you develop a better understanding of your roles. Some of the behaviors the two of you should identify within yourselves to cope with include self-depreciation, people-pleasing, unclear and unfollowed boundaries, excessive caring/enabling, and the urge to act out on intense, unpleasant emotions.

An excellent way to get started is for each of you to keep a journal where you'll both write down how you experience a situation and then compare notes. When it comes to setting up your journal, make sure you separate the page into five distinct columns, with each labeled as situations, thoughts, emotions, behaviors, and alternative thoughts.

In the situations column, you will want to write down all the target experiences you've encountered throughout the day that is as devoid of all emotion as possible. Using facts alone is critical, as anything else will skew the entire process.

For the column labeled thoughts, you want to include the thoughts that the experience caused and what feelings they led to. These thoughts may be statements, questions or a bit of both, but regardless, it's crucial to the process that you are honest with yourself about what you're thinking, as doing otherwise will taint your results.

For the emotions column, you want to consider more than just how you felt; you're going to focus on one or two emotions that seemed as though they really ruled the day. It's important to take your time, as snap judgments are only going to lead to the wrong identification of base emotions like anger and sadness when more complicated shades of these emotions are to blame.

For the behaviors column, you will write down the way you responded to the situation at the moment. Make sure you write down exactly how you responded in the situation, not the way you would have liked to respond, or the way you would have responded upon further consideration. You will also include in this column the way your action affected the situation as well.

Finally, in the column labeled alternative thoughts, you will list the sorts of things you could have done at the moment to ensure that things took on a more productive outcome. Don't feel bad if, at the start, you end up leaving this column blank; better ways to handle anxious situations will become apparent in time. The types of things you put into this column should be practical tips and tricks that you have learned from experience or other sources, but it should also be a space for additional brainstorming.

Setting Boundaries

Codependent people have trouble setting boundaries for two reasons: 1) they don't want to create conflict between themselves and a person they're close to, and 2) they feel so much love and compassion towards the other person that they're willing to put up with almost anything.

A lack of boundaries is a sure sign of a codependent relationship. Without having a well-defined boundary as to what you are and aren't willing to put up with, the relationship with the person you're with can quickly spiral into toxicity. Furthermore, it can also allow both yourself and your partner to indulge in unchecked self-destructive behavior.

It can be challenging to set boundaries with people who have a domineering personality. Constant taunting, testing, protesting, or pleading can quickly wear out your resolution, especially if you're already prone to codependency. However, while the lack of boundaries may make the relationship seem more free and exciting at first, it's only a matter of time before you find yourself wishing you had set them in the beginning.

Codependents usually don't have much experience in setting boundaries. Even worse, they may feel as though they don't have the right to set boundaries, as their self-worth is so closely tied to the opinion their partner has of them.

A relationship with boundaries is typically much healthier and more sustainable than one without. Having boundaries fosters a relationship in which the desires, needs, and interests of both parties are fairly represented, recognized, and heard. Research suggests that having boundaries can improve the level of happiness in both parties because their clear presence gives the people in the relationship an idea of what is acceptable and what isn't. This, along with the knowledge that their partner understands their needs and concerns does a tremendous job of eliminating stress and anxiety.

Enforcing Boundaries

Setting boundaries can be hard, especially if you're not used to the idea. Even the very act of setting boundaries itself can often be unpleasant. By setting a boundary with someone you're in a relationship with, you are inadvertently telling them that they did or have been doing something that you're uncomfortable with, and this can make your partner feel awful. It can also be unpleasant for you emotionally because setting a boundary involves acknowledging that you are in a relationship with a person who is selfish, invasive, or inconsiderate enough to prompt you to draw the line.

So how should we go about setting boundaries? Well, there's not exactly a perfect and easy way. However, there are some basic things you can do to help make the process as smooth and painless as possible.

The first thing you should do when setting a boundary is to establish the importance of it to yourself. Usually, this is done by thinking back to specific incidents that made you feel uncomfortable, hurt, violated, or any other type of negative emotion that could have been prevented had there been a clear boundary set in place. Go through these incidents and think of the reasons why they occurred. What made your partner act that way? What do you think prompted them to do this? Do you think they knew that this action would make you feel the way you did? Or did they just do it without thinking over their decision, unaware of how it would affect you?

Usually, people do things that negatively affect their partner without realizing it. This is why after you've identified a specific boundary, you have to go through all the reasons why you need it. This involves gathering information about how it made you feel and why it made you feel that way.

The next thing you should do before you finally bring up the boundary with your partner is to prepare yourself for how they might react. A small conflict might emerge over the validity of the boundary, so you need to have the reasons you gathered for it ready to go. There's also a chance that you setting this boundary may cause your partner to be unhappy with you for a while after you bring it up. But if they show a significant amount of resistance to a modest, reasonable boundary, then there may be further problems in your relationship. In a vast majority of cases, however, although the partner will be a little upset for a while, a good partner will come to accept it out of respect for you. Setting a boundary is a good test to determine exactly how much your partner respects your needs.

So now it's time to bring up the boundary with your partner. While you can't control exactly how this conversation will go, there are a few basic things you can do to make the road less bumpy. First, bring up the topic at a time when they're not busy. People listen better and are most understanding when they are relaxed and not stressed. So make sure the two of you are in a calm, stress-free environment.

Now you need to communicate your thoughts clearly. Give them the exact reasons why you feel this boundary should be established. Lay them out in a clear, concise manner and leave room for them to ask questions. It's important to place the focus on how you feel, not on what they did. You don't want them to feel as though their behavior was malicious or horrific. The best thing to do is to explain how you feel about these issues and how you would like them to improve. Approach them calmly and don't accuse them of purposely trying to hurt you. It's likely that the need to set a boundary came about because of a simple misunderstanding or ignorance of your emotions. However, if you do think they did something to hurt you intentionally, you might need to take a different course of action that's a little more radical than setting boundaries.

Examples of poor boundaries include:

"You can't go out with your friends without me. You know how jealous I get. You have to stay home with me."

"Sorry guys, I can't go out with you tonight; my girl-friend gets really angry when I go out without her."

"My co-workers are idiots, and I'm always late to meetings because I have to tell them how to do their jobs."

"I'd love to take that job in Milwaukee, but my mother would never forgive me for moving so far away."

"I can date you, but can you not tell my friend Cindy? She gets really jealous when I have a boyfriend and she doesn't."

In each scenario, the person is either taking responsibility for someone else's actions, or they are demanding that someone else take responsibility for their actions.

The following scenario comes up in codependent friendships: A long-time friend screws up, but instead of taking personal responsibility, they expect you to shoulder some of the responsibility with them because "that's what friends do."

"Hey Jill, you and I have been working side by side for over four years. I can't believe you would say that to our boss without talking to me about it first."

"But the data you added to the sheet was wrong because you didn't double check the numbers. You know how important it was we got everything right by the deadline."

"Even still, you should have backed me up instead of disagreeing with me in front of everyone."

"Look, we're friends, and you know that I value your friendship, but I'm not going to do your work for you. I'm sorry, but that's the end of the discussion.

"I'm doing my job just fine."

"Well, then my comments shouldn't really matter."

This next example is of a codependent relationship from a partner's view who is often smothered or pampered too much.

"You know that new job you were thinking about looking for? Well, I started putting in a good word for you with the HR department at my company."

"Thanks...but you didn't have to do that."

"Well, I wanted to! You know I just want you to be successful. I was also thinking about us moving in together again. I know this really great two bedroom apartment that just opened up down the street."

"I told you that I don't think we are ready for that yet."

"How much longer do you want to wait? We aren't getting any younger after all. Why don't we just try it?"

"Last month you replaced half my clothes with things you thought I would like, now you want us to work and live together as well?"

"You know I love you; I just want to take care of you."

"I love you too, but you have to let me do things my own way. This is not healthy. You taking control of my life decisions without consulting me first."

"I can't believe how selfish you are! I do EVERYTHING for you and now you're blaming me for it!"

"If you really care about me, then you need to stop trying to control my life and let me live it on my own."

Following Boundaries

The existence of a boundary doesn't mean much if it's not followed. Right after a boundary is set, it's sometimes normal to have a grace period in which your partner is given a chance to adjust to it, but a kind and understanding partner will change their behavior very quickly when they learn that something is bothering you.

But it's not only up to your partner to maintain the boundary. This is especially true for boundaries that have a muddy grey area in which it isn't too clear what's acceptable and what isn't. For the sake of understanding and communication, you should make the borderline of the boundary clear.

In the course of living within a relationship that has a set boundary, you have to remind yourself the reasons why you decided that you needed this boundary in the first place from time to time, or at least as often as the issue comes up. This will strengthen your resolve if the boundary is questioned down the line.

Another thing you want to do while trying to maintain a boundary is not to let your partner get away with crossing it. If it's a clear, well-defined boundary, there's likely no reason why your partner should "accidentally" cross it or forget about it. If they do, it means one of two things: 1) they don't have enough of a concern for your needs to remember a simple boundary you've clearly asked them not to cross, or 2) they are aware of the boundary and simply don't feel the need to follow it because they either want to cause you discomfort or think it's "no big deal." Both reasons are problematic and may indicate deeper problems within your relationship.

When to Escalate

Entering the waters that involve ending a relationship is probably one of the most challenging things people find themselves having to do. Although it's often ugly and unpleasant, it's also necessary. The circumstances and emotions within a codependent relationship are usually much more complicated than relationships other people ever have to deal with. Likely, there will be a ton of factors to consider. Some of these will ring out to you as warning bells telling you to end the relationship, but others might tug on your heart hard enough to tell you that you should stay. It can be tough to sort through these different variables and truly know which path to follow. So in the following paragraphs, we'll discuss some sure signs that it's time to move on.

One of the most common reasons a person will stay in a toxic, codependent relationship that shows little signs of improvement is not because they love and want to take care of the other person, but because they don't want to be alone. A fear of abandonment can be a powerful motivator to keep yourself subjected to something that does more harm than good. An excellent way to decide if it's time to leave is to take a step back and honestly consider why you are still in the relationship. Is it your love for them? Or are you terrified of being alone? Often people stay in relationships like these due to unpleasant break-ups they've gone through in the past, and they'll do anything, no matter how much it hurts them, to save themselves from experiencing that again.

Another good sign that it's time to move on is if you've been trying to work on the issues in your relationship for a while, and it shows no signs of improving. As stated above, you cannot help someone who neither believes they have a problem or wants to change. If you've been aware of your relationship's codependency for a while and your partner shows no signs of changing, it might be time to think about leaving. After all, if you stay in a relationship that does more harm than good, it can be easy to put it off to avoid pain. And if you're not careful, this can waste months or even years of your life.

Should You Quit Social Media?

While codependency is mainly the result of a dysfunctional upbringing, many other factors can encourage codependent behavior. There are many things in this world that, while not meaning to encourage codependence, do discourage independence. The world that we live in today is the most connected mass community in human history. Although it has become easier to tune into and communicate with other people, it's also become harder to exist independently of other people. While eliminating these factors won't help most people suffering from codependency recover, it will help them identify the influences that may foster a mindset of codependency.

There are two main ways that social media encourages codependency: 1) it makes it easier to stay in touch with people whom you may have had a toxic relationship with in the past, and 2) it gives a person's codependent needs a tool for getting affection, acceptance, and approval.

As we'll learn later, one of the very first things you have to do when recovering from codependency is to cut the person you were in a codependent relationship with out of your life. Twenty years ago, this meant losing their number, avoiding them in person, ignoring their emails, and getting rid of everything you had that was associated with them. Now, it means deleting their number, photos, and voicemails, and blocking them on Snapchat, Twitter,

JEAN HARRISON, BEATTIE GREY

Facebook, Instagram, and a lot more, depending on how technologically active you are.

However, even if you block their phone number, they can get a messaging app and connect with you that way. So, if it's imperative that you have absolutely no contact with them, you might have to go as far as changing your number. Social media has given codependents a hundred new ways to hang on to the past. In the same way that it makes it easier to communicate, it makes it just as difficult to separate.

Social media also gives credence to the unhealthy obsession codependents have in the acceptance of others; only now, their need for approval can be measured in the forms of likes, retweets, or any other type of engagement on social media. Not only has this become much easier to do, but it's also encouraged. Today, it's normal to measure someone's self-worth by how many followers they have or how much attention their posts get.

For someone prone to codependency, this is a blessing and a curse. If you know how to post the right things, you'll get more followers and attention. So a codependent person might get some satisfaction out of their social media presence in that sense. However, it's far more detrimental in the long run. It not only enables them to value themselves based on other people's opinions, but it also instills the idea that it's healthy and okay to rely so much on other people's opinions to feel good about yourself, which is not the case.

When it comes to breaking free from social media, first you'll need to make sure that you set the correct boundaries. These boundaries will vary depending on the individual; some might be able to see an occasional post from their ex without issue, while others will need to go full social media blackout. Next, focus on moving forward by unfollowing the person or blocking them, as this will allow you to cut them off entirely.

NINE

Healing From Codependency

RECOVERY, WHETHER IN YOUR own habits or within your relationships, must begin with your transformation. To make any progress in the quality of your relationships, you have to take an honest look at your own problems and work towards correcting those them.

Using Affirmations to Facilitate Recovery

Recovery, whether in your own habits or within your relationships, must begin with transformation. To make any progress in the quality of your relationships, you have to take an honest look at your own problems and work towards correcting them.

One of the simplest and easiest things you can do to start recovering from codependency is to use affirmations to strengthen your sense of self, independence, and confidence. This is a great tool to use in your recovery, as you can use them anytime, anywhere.

Affirmations are statements you can use to nurture yourself and increase your self-confidence. You can say them out loud, write them down, or just think them.

A common problem people with codependency struggle with is negative and intrusive thoughts. This occurs unconsciously and is often learned over a lifetime of adapting to toxic environments. Often, these come automatically and have a tendency not only to make situations seem hopeless but also turn us into pessimists who always look at the dark side of things.

Affirmations are a tool to counteract this habit. Not only can it help you cope with difficult situations, but when used correctly and reinforced over time, it can change your outlook on life and train your mind to think positive thoughts automatically.

Before you start using affirmations, you must first develop a certain degree of mindfulness. This is a simple technique that involves learning to identify the negative thoughts in your mind. At first, it may take a lot of effort, and you'll likely find yourself caught in negative thoughts (if you are prone to them) without being conscious of them. This is normal. Just set aside time to practice being aware of these negative thoughts daily, which can be done in traffic, in the shower, at work, watching TV, or literally during any other passive activity.

Once you can identify these negative thoughts, corner them, focus on them, and replace them with positive thoughts. For example, if you have anxiety over a project at work and you hear yourself saying that it's going to turn out poorly, then pause, identify the thought, focus on it, and let it float away. Then tell yourself that the project is going to be a success.

Like all other skills, using affirmations is going to be challenging and ineffective at first. But as you keep using them, you'll notice that two things start to happen. First, they will be easier to use and start coming naturally. Second, they'll become more effective, and you'll automatically use them when a negative thought shows up.

Here are some suggestions for affirmations that you can use.

- I deserve love, kindness, and tenderness.

- I am a good person.

- I try my best to support myself and those around

me with love and affection, and I deserve that same level of affection back.

- I am good at many things.

- I am not the mistakes I have made in my past.

- I try my best at everything I do to the extent that my mind, body, and energy allow me.

- I can trust my own opinions.

- I am a pleasant person to be around.

- I am in control of my life.

- I have obstacles and issues just like everyone else. They are not at the center of my life. They do not control my life. And they do not control me.

Of course, there are many, many more kinds of affirmations you can use. You can find them with a simple google search. I'd suggest finding a long list of them and picking out a few that especially applies to you..

What Honesty Means

Honesty is often type-casted as something that is exclusively between you and someone else. This aspect of honesty is a good interpersonal attribute to have when it comes to intimate relationships, but in the sphere of codependency recovery, the best kind of honesty is the one you have towards yourself. It can be very tempting, especially for someone suffering from codependent tendencies, to ignore, skew, or rationalize their own problems. For people who have a solid stance to begin working towards recovery, one of the first things they can do to help themselves is to learn how to be honest with themselves.

To see if you're ready to begin this, you should first prepare for it by getting into the right mindset to do an honest session of self-reflection. You should be calm, and to an extent, distant from your emotions so that you can look at yourself through an objective lens. Doing this allows you to look at yourself and your issues without feeling an overwhelming sense of guilt, shame, or regret.

Once you're confident that you're in the right mindset, make sure you're alone in your environment. It should be a place you're familiar with that's quiet and peaceful where you can spend a good amount of time without being disturbed.

Once all this is set, you can begin. It's good to work your way through the minor issues before moving onto those that are more emotionally charged. You can also start by focusing on yourself and the positive aspects that you're proud of. This puts you into a positive mindset by motivating you to continue, builds a sense of rapport with your own judgment by examining your qualities, and qualifies you to move on to more serious issues.

While you're thinking about your issues, try to break them down and identify behaviors that led to them, and then go even further by identifying thoughts and emotions that led to them.

Once these issues and their cause start to make sense, it can be helpful to write down specific epiphanies to come back to later. This ensures you won't forget about the things you realized about yourself and that they won't get warped in your memory. The statements or realizations you write down should be focused. If you have something that's wide and expansive, break it down into separate aspects and focus on them individually. Also, you shouldn't just stop at thinking of behaviors you can improve on. Instead, you should write out what that behavior is, what it means for the outer situation, and some possible steps you should take to reach it.

Becoming Your Own Person

This is perhaps the most crucial aspect of recovery from codependency. One of the thickest roots of codependency is a weak sense of self, and it can make us attach ourselves to other people. Because of this, we might have a hard time deciding what we want and instead, will worry about what others want of us. Instead of drawing boundaries, we may allow people to do things that make us uncomfortable just because we are so afraid of them leaving.

Being your own person starts with the little things, from what you decide to wear in the morning to what you choose to do on the weekends. When picking out your clothes before you start the day, dress according to how you want to look and how you wish to express yourself, not to conform with the latest fashion trend or how you think others want you to look. Don't put off getting tattoos, piercings, or other forms of self-expression because you're afraid of what people will think. Do it because you want to and you think they reflect your inner self.

Another thing you can do to become your own person is to be open to new experiences. How do you know you like something if you've never tried it? Does it sound scary? Challenging? Good! New experiences bring you outside of your comfort zone and put you into situations that can help you figure out who you are. It also makes you more confident in your abilities.

Also, try to be more assertive in social situations by using more "I" statements. Statements like "I feel," or "I want" allow you to get your point across in a clear and effective way. By including the word "I," you make it clear to the other person that their viewpoint is as valid as your own. Additionally, it will help you keep the facts separate from what you want out of a given situation, which will ensure that you come to the best outcome possible.

A lot of people who struggle with codependency have trouble taking control of situations. And while you don't always want to do this, it can be a big plus to voice your desires with a healthy confidence and authority. It decreases the odds you'll get into situations you didn't want to be in. Likewise, it makes the time you spend with other people more enjoyable because you'll be engaging in activities that you prefer.

TEN

A Guide to Self-Care

L IKE WITH ANY MENTAL issue, codependency can cause large amounts of distress for those affected. While codependency isn't physically harmful in itself, it can often lead to people neglecting their health and well-being. They may let their financial situation rupture. Sometimes, their homes come into a state of total disarray. They eat foods that are bad for them and don't practice good hygiene. It's also not uncommon for codependents to turn towards drugs or alcohol to escape the emotional pain they're in.

Besides having the potential to decrease someone's quality of life significantly, someone who neglects their health is simultaneously constructing a roadblock on their path to recovery. Healing from codependency, like any other type of mental issue, requires more than a healthy, robust level of support. A codependent person also needs an immense amount of willpower to overcome their problematic behaviors as they are often extremely deep-rooted and sometimes inseparable from their personality.

Before recovery can begin, a person must learn to take care of themselves. When someone isn't caring for themselves at all, it's hard to muster the energy for recovery; it can also be very difficult for them to stick to a strategy. Recovery from codependency requires a baseline of good health, as well as a basic knowledge of how to cope with negative emotions.

Empathy and Self-Awareness

A big problem codependent people face is that they're so used to taking care of others that taking care of themselves is a foreign concept. Often they devote a lot of energy to taking care of someone in the hopes that they'll receive the same amount of effort in return. This step is especially important for codependents to take because the iron core of codependent behavior is a radically fluctuating idea of self-worth. When someone doesn't believe that they're likable, good, or worthy of kindness or love, they will have a hard time practicing self-care and treating themselves with kindness.

Before they can begin, the person must establish that they are worthy of self-care. No magic ritual or sentence will give someone the boost in self-esteem they need to practice self-care. Building rapport with yourself is a rather long process which requires much effort. However, there are a few "thought exercises" you can start doing right now that can help you begin to take the steps towards having a healthy concept of your self-worth.

The first is to expand the image you have of yourself. It's easier to feel undeserving when you're just taking into consideration the state of your life as it is. In this mindset, if your surrounding environment is terrible, then it's common to see it as a reflection of yourself. But when we do this, we are only looking at a tiny sliver of our time on this planet. You are not fixed into place like an object, and you didn't choose to be placed in your current situation.

An exercise that will help you develop empathy is to recap the history of your life. First, go year by year, beginning with your birth. Though you probably won't remember anything until around five years old, take the time to pause and reflect on who you were at this time. Think back to when you were a baby once, how you couldn't talk, depended on your caretakers for everything, and knew nothing at all about the world. Next, think about when you were two and how the only thing you knew about the world was what you were shown or told. Reflect on the time when you were three and knew a little bit more, could move around on your own, and communicate with your parents.

Then go to age four, then five, then six, and so on. Go through your memories as best you can. Think about positive memories, negative memories, and everything in between. Go through every year until you reach your present age. The purpose of this exercise to teach you that you came into this world without asking to be here, not knowing anything, and are a product of your experiences and nothing else. You were a blank slate, and you still are a slate, only now, it's covered with random markings and symbols.

Another way to practice empathy and kindness is to imagine yourself as an outsider and stranger. Go over everything you're dealing with and experienced. Then try to imagine that someone you know has all the same aspects and experiences as you, and try to love this person the same way you would love someone you respect.

These exercises may not work the first few times you try them, but if you keep at it, you'll find yourself developing a fresh and new perspective of who you are. Once you start making progress, chances are you'll be surprised at how hard you were on yourself.

Getting Rest

A majority of the population is aware that getting an adequate amount of sleep is ideal for good health, but it may surprise you to know exactly how much a good night's rest can help. The CDC estimates that about thirty percent of Americans are running on six hours of sleep or less. In response, many people might say that they feel fine on six hours and don't need anymore. But the reality is that while there are individuals whose genetic makeup allows them to feel rested on less sleep, this is true for only about five percent of Americans. So, if you're getting fewer than six hours of sleep regularly, chances are you're sleep deprived.

To demonstrate how important sleep is to your health, we'll present you with some facts. The Beck Depression Inventory (BDI) is a twenty-one question self-report that is used by mental health professionals to determine how depressed an individual is. It is scored from zero to sixty-three, with sixty-three indicating the highest level of depression. It's been used in different experiments over the years. When the first selective serotonin reuptake inhibitor (SSRI) anti-depressant (Prozac) was developed in the 1980s, the BDI was one of the tools they used to assess the effectiveness of the new drug. What they found, when they accounted for the placebo effect and other variables, was that the anti-depressant reduced a patient's BDI score by one point.

On the other hand, when researchers did a study of how sleeping habits affected depression, they studied people who went from sleeping six or fewer hours per night to eight or more. They had them fill out the BDI before the study began and again after it ended. They found that getting an adequate amount of sleep after being chronically sleep-deprived raised the patients' BDI score by seven points.

A few dangers of chronic sleep deprivation include a significantly increased chance of developing Alzheimer's, heart disease, various types of cancers, certain auto-immune diseases, heart attacks, stroke, arthritis, and countless others. But the effect of healthier sleeping habits on a patient's BDI score should get the point across.

So now that we've established just how important sleep is both to our mental and physical health, it's time to take action. But taking steps to improve your sleeping habits can be rather hard. A busy life can force you to choose between getting a good night sleep and working late on a project. Also, stress from codependency or other personal issues can affect sleep quality, making it difficult falling and staying asleep.

There are a few things you can do to get more sleep. You can organize your responsibilities to be more efficient, giving yourself more free time you can allocate toward sleep. If that's not an option, you can also try to find an hour or two during the day when you can take a nap.

When it comes to falling asleep, it's important to stay away from sleeping pills, even over the counter ones. You can build up a dependence on any drug, and it can be very tempting to use them every night. The problem with this is that it will eventually stop working as you build a tolerance, causing you to take more in order to achieve the same effect. However, there are many natural supplements that can help, such as magnesium, passion flower, valerian root, lavender, glycine, and ashwagandha.

You can also help yourself fall asleep by adjusting the temperature of the room you're sleeping in, preferably around sixty-five degrees. Also, computer screens emit blue light, which gives a signal to our brains that the sun is out and it's time to wake up, leading to insomnia when we browse our screens right before bed. To prevent this, try not to look at any screens an hour before bed, or search for programs or apps you can download that will filter out the blue light on your phone or computer. You should also aim to exercise regularly. Being physically tired gives your brain a clear signal that it's time to sleep at the end of the day.

Dealing with Stress

Like with any mental issue, chances are that dealing with and experiencing codependency is going to be a very stressful experience. Again, there is no magic rule of self-care that will eliminate stress, but there are some basic things you can do to help yourself deal with stress.

The first is to maintain a healthy network of social support. One of the mistakes codependents often make when they begin recovery is cutting off communication with their social network. Not only can this be unhealthy, but it also doesn't facilitate recovery. It's important to maintain relationships because they are a vital part of a healthy, joyful life. Seeking support doesn't mean that your friends become your therapists. It simply means that you have people in your life who like to be around you as much as you like being around them.

Another way of coping with stress is by dealing with the source of the problem itself. If you have a project due or bills to pay, work out how you're going to accomplish these tasks. If you just ignore a problem and stress about it, you're letting that it have control over you. However, when you sit down to figure out how you're going to solve it, you gain control over the situation, and nothing will catch you off guard. Studies show that we produce more stress hormones when we're lying in bed not doing anything than when we're actually working.

Another good way to deal with stress is to engage in a hobby or therapeutic activity that you enjoy. Often, when you're in a stressful position and under the pressure of having to make important decisions, it can be incredibly relaxing to do a simple task that doesn't require much thinking, such as building Legos, knitting, or any other repetitive, simple activity.

Overcoming Negative Emotions

A big part of self-care is learning how to cope with negative emotions. Usually, the people who experience the most intense emotions have the least knowledge on how to deal with them. Sometimes negative emotions can cause us so much pain that we will go to great lengths to escape them, such as engaging in substance abuse, destructive behavior, self-harm, and other unhealthy coping mechanisms.

Thinking that it's possible to go through life without ever experiencing pain is dangerous.

Knowing this establishes the importance of learning how to deal with painful emotions and planning for them when they occur. A person who knows how to do this successfully has a few advantages: more control over their lives, a detachment from their emotions, and the ability to make rational decisions in emotionally charged situations.

A fundamental principle we should discuss here is how you should react when you encounter negative emotions. When we feel an intense emotion, we have two options: We can either let it control us, or we can simply acknowledge it, observe it, and let it drift away. Sometimes, emotions may be so powerful that this may seem impossible at first, but it will work over time. By doing this exercise, you're flexing a muscle that you've probably never used before. So, the more you flex and exercise it, the stronger it will get.

Something else you can do when experiencing painful emotions is to practice something called TIP chemistry. Explaining the acronym makes it more confusing than it needs to be, but the basic concept is that you can distract your mind from painful emotions by exposing your body to intense sensations. These sensations give you a "shock," which is really a wave of endorphins being re-leased throughout your body. There are two main ways of doing this. The first is to splash cold water on your face, preferably a sink, but a cup with ice water works as well. The second is to hold an ice cube in your hand for about ten to fifteen seconds. While these exercises won't take away the emotion completely, they can provide a quick solution to the problem.

Organize and Keep Yourself Healthy

There are many benefits to organizing your life and keep-ing yourself healthy. This will help eliminate any stress that comes from clutter. As a result, you will be prepared for all of your future obligations, you can plan out your finances to make sure you and your family are taken care of, and you'll lose things a lot less often.

Studies have shown that doing something as simple as cleaning your room can significantly change your mood. People are more productive in clean rooms due to less clutter. There are also benefits in doing little things such as making your bed. It's a fact that most people don't make their bed in the morning. The most common reason is that they feel they're above doing something so small. But this is often the first step to a more structured, organized, and productive life. By taking on smaller responsibilities, you prepare yourself to organize and take control of more challenging tasks.

Another important aspect of self-care is keeping yourself healthy. A balanced diet and regular exercise are just as important to your mental health as it is to your physical health. By being healthy, you'll have more energy to improve other aspects of your life. It also boosts your self-esteem quite a bit by giving you a sense of accomplishment..

Sorry to interrupt again, but...

Are you enjoying this book? If so, then I'd love to hear your thoughts!

As an independent author with a tiny marketing budget, I rely on readers, like you, to leave a short review on Amazon.

Even if it's just a sentence or two!

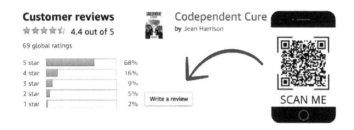

So if you enjoyed the book, please...

>> Visit www.TitleRatings.com/Codependent or **scan the QR code above** to be taken directly to the Amazon review page.

I personally read every review, so leave me a little message.

I'd like to thank you from the bottom of my heart for purchasing this book and making it this far. And now, move on to the next page to the final chapter!

ELEVEN

The Road to Recovery

RECOVERING FROM CODEPENDENCY IS a long road in and of itself, but often the struggle extends far beyond the time you find yourself getting better. For those who have spent extended periods in toxic environments or were raised in broken homes, it might be easy to fall into the same habits if you're not careful. Maintaining recovery from codependency includes making sure you take care of yourself, identifying and learning how to cope with your triggers, and maintaining a healthy state of mindfulness.

Supporting Yourself

Someone capable of being independent looks much different than someone obsessed with it. They are okay with being alone for months, spending weekends at home, and getting by with the support of no one but themselves. This is a good characteristic to have. It gives you the ability to choose whom you enter relationships with, and you won't become instantly overly dependent on them. It allows you to take a step back, collect yourself, and leave relationships that are toxic.

At the same time, it's also good to take care of yourself physically. You don't have to be a health freak or be in really good shape, but you should make an effort to be healthy. Depression and anxiety have a tendency to move in when people aren't taking care of themselves. Empty calories and refined sugars don't necessarily need to be completely avoided, but you also shouldn't eat too much of them.

Identifying Pressure Points

Once you've recovered from codependency, you'll naturally notice certain situations that put you at risk for spiraling back into old habits. Often, they can cause you a significant amount of emotional distress. When they happen, emotions can get intense and very unpleasant. So it's essential to identify them and find ways to avoid them in the future. However, you may have triggers that are a part of everyday life and cannot be avoided. For these, make sure you have a plan in place for how to cope with them.

There are a few different ways to identify pressure points. First, take some time to write down the things that have happened in your past that led to undesirable outcomes. When you think back on these, try to remember what was happening in your life towards the very beginning of the event. Sometimes, these pressure points can seem very casual, but whatever they are, identifying them will make sure that you aren't caught off guard when unfortunate circumstances occur.

Mindfulness

Since its inception, mindfulness meditation has been proven through scientific study to improve the physical wellbeing of those that practice it regularly. At its heart, mindfulness meditation is all about focusing your mind on being fully present in each moment, which allows you to exist entirely in any given moment by expanding your consciousness to the fullest.

Mindfulness is the practice of controlling where your mind goes. It involves separating yourself from negative emotions about the past or future and taking in what you are currently experiencing in your current state of mind. The end goal of mindfulness is to prevent being controlled by your emotions. Because mindfulness is a skill, if you're not used to it, then you may have trouble making it work for you in the beginning. Therefore, you should practice it often to improve its effectiveness.

Mindfulness is a form of meditation. Hence, you need to ensure that you're free of any distractions. During this process, feel the air on your skin and the temperature of the room. Distance yourself from your thoughts by acknowledging them and the emotions that come with it, and letting them drift away.

A good way to introduce yourself to this practice is to look up a few guided mindfulness meditation videos on YouTube. They're very effective for when you're experiencing intense emotions and having trouble controlling them. You can also find great guides on mindfulness with a simple google search.

TWELVE

Conclusion

C ODEPENDENCY AFFECTS MANY PEOPLE. Whether it's very serious or subtle, it's usually always a problem. No one is ever at fault for having codependency. In life, we encounter many situations we don't anticipate, but it's our responsibility to deal with them.

Someone prone to codependency more often than not had an upbringing that wasn't properly nurturing or supportive. And often, they learn to use codependency as a way to gain the affection they were deprived of in childhood.

I hope this book was helpful and that through the course of reading it, you have come to a deeper understanding of codependent behaviors either in yourself or others around you. Lastly, I hope it has given you the perspective you need to begin working towards healing and recovery.

Remember that you can come back to this book at any time to refresh your memory or seek guidance.

Enjoyed this book? Don't miss out on the next installment in the series on the following page.

Don't Miss Out On The Next Book In This Series

If you found "Codependent Cure" helpful, you should definitely check out the next book in this series called **"Narcissist Abuse Recovery."**

No matter how far you've come on your journey to recovery, an encounter with the narcissist can be devastating to your progress.

We briefly explored the subject of narcissism in this book, emphasizing its grave implications that demand your attention. Becoming entangled in a toxic relationship with a narcissist has the potential to undo all the progress you've achieved in the blink of an eye.

So, what's the plan to protect your recovery? That's where this essential guide comes in.

It equips you with the necessary tools to understand the inner workings of narcissists, enabling you to break free from abusive relationships so that you can stop gravitating towards self-absorbed people who could care less about you.

Victims are often left shattered and without a voice because they feel that no one could possibly believe or understand the suffering they are silently enduring. However, it is entirely possible to reclaim your power from a narcissist, attain liberation, and rediscover your true self with a renewed sense of purpose!

Take this crucial step toward your healing journey by visiting **www.BonusGuides.com/Narcissist** or scan the QR code in the image to secure your copy today!

Printed in Great Britain
by Amazon

40186616R10072